# INDEX

**Minaret Bracelet**
pages 6 - 8

**Angles Bracelets**
pages 9 - 11

**Patchwork Bracelets**
pages 12 - 14

**Window Bracelets**
pages 15 - 18

**Glitzy Button Bracelets**
pages 19 - 21

**Egyptian Wave Bracelet**
pages 22 - 24

**Pleated Bracelet**
pages 25 - 28

**Beaded Beads**
pages 29 - 35

# Alice Korach

*Alice Korach is the founding editor of Bead&Button Magazine. Her idea in starting the magazine was that there were many people like her who wanted to know how beautiful beadwork was created, and she was right!*

*From childhood on, Alice practiced almost all forms of needle art, taking up beading when she was eight and knitting at eleven. She always loved teaching and sharing her skills and knowledge with others. In her first career, Alice earned a Ph.D. in English literature and became a college professor. The biggest problem with academia for her was that one was required to write uninteresting articles for a limited audience of hostile specialists.*

*So Alice moved on to Threads Magazine where she was an editor in all areas of fiber arts, particularly knitting, and contributed numerous articles of her own work, most notably, the first article explaining bead knitting since the early years of the 20th century.*

*Alice always knew that she was a good technician and a skilled designer, but she only gradually learned that she was also an artist when she had the privilege of learning pâte de verre from Donna Milliron. Alice went on to create dozens of unique three-dimensional glass sculptures including figurative, abstract, and floral works. Practicing art in glass freed something within her that has led to an artistic flowering in other forms of bead art as well.*

*Alice teaches at national conventions and shops, particularly at the 'Bead Needs' shop in Hales Corners, Wisconsin.*

*www.LostWaxGlass.com*
LMK467@earthlink.net          262-650-0574
Alice Korach,  518 McCall St., Waukesha, WI 53186

## Bead Shapes and Sizes

Unusual beads are great to work with. In this book I focused on special shaped beads. They are a lot of fun to work with and give an unusual look to ordinary stitches.

Cube Beads: Left, 4mm "oil slick" luster and raku finish matte metallic; center, 3mm silver-lined and matte opaque; right, 2mm raku finish (2 beads); far right, 14/0 round seed beads for comparison.

## Cube Beads

Cube beads from Toho are available in four sizes: 1.5mm, 2mm, 3mm, and 4mm. Most Toho cubes have a large slightly diamond-shaped hole; while Miyuki cubes have a large round hole. Finishes range from matte to shiny, opaque, transparent, silver- or color-lined, metallic and luster or aurora borealis (AB).

The 4mm cubes are the easiest size to find. They work well for most projects, but may be a bit too big for a bracelet or a small piece with design details. I really like using the 3mm size because they're small enough to allow room for a bit of embellishment or other design detailing, but they're large enough to present a strong cube shape.

The smallest cubes are about 1.5mm on a side, or about the size of a 15/0 round seed bead. At this size, the cubic form isn't as clear, but if you can find a wide enough range of colors, you can create detailed charted patterns that fit together like a precisely constructed brick road or a micro mosaic.

Triangle Beads: Top left, size 14/0 purple/bronze metallic; center and bottom left, size 11/0 color-lined crystal and "oil slick" luster metallic; top and center right, size 8/0 matte metallic AB and metallic bronze iris; bottom right, size 5/0 color-lined crystal.

## Triangle Beads

Triangle beads from Toho are known for their sharp corners; while Miyuki triangles have rounded corners. Toho triangles come in sizes 14/0, 11/0, 8/0, and 5/0. These sizes correspond to round seed beads in terms of the width of the bead across the hole, but they are significantly longer than their round counterparts. You'll find the widest color and finish range in 11/0 triangles, which have been made the longest. But 8/0 triangles are coming along fast and many come in the same or coordinating colors as 11/0s, which creates a lot of design options.

You'll also find a fair amount of irregularity in a package of triangle beads of any size. In some of the designs in this book, I'll suggest that you carefully sort through your triangle beads for uniform beads, but the "Egyptian Wave" and "Pleated" bracelets only work if you take advantage of size variation to pick beads that fill enlarging or shrinking spaces, depending on where you are in the pattern.

Strangely, some colors of triangles have smooth, fire-polished edges, while others seem to be cut like bugles and often present sharp or irregular edges. These are a bit riskier to use, but the colors are irresistible, so cull out those with the roughest edges and reserve them for stringing or fringe.

## Threads

You should, of course, use your favorite needles and threads. Many beaders swear by the strength of Fireline, but I haven't used it since a piece I'd woven on Fireline came apart in a million pieces. I was a Nymo beader until very recently when Toho and Kobayashi both introduced the same new nylon filament thread in slightly different palettes. Toho's thread is called One-G and Kobayashi's is K-O. The weight is similar to Nymo B, but the thread has a slick coating that causes it to resist fraying without needing any type of thread conditioner (beeswax or Thread Heaven). It also seems to be comparable in strength to Nymo D.

One-G and K-O need to be prestretched before you begin to weave. This thread is very stretchy, so prestretching will prevent your beadwork from becoming loose over time. It also uncoils the thread, which helps minimize tangling. As with any thread, you should thread the needle with the end that comes off the spool first so you are sewing with the thread's grain to minimize fraying. I am a lazy beader and tend to use excessively long threads. This is a false economy of time because a thread longer than 2 yd. (1.8m) is much more likely to tangle.

If you are using beads with sharp edges, such as crystals or some 11/0 triangles, you may prefer to use Fireline or Power Pro (BeadCats sells a generic version of the latter at a much reduced price). I used One-G and K-O for all the projects in this book.

## Needles

Since cubes and triangles have large holes, most of the projects in this book can be worked with size 10 English beading needles.

You may need to use a size 12 needle for projects that involve extra thread passes, such as the "Beaded Beads" necklace.

## Scissors and Glue

My favorite beading scissors are high-quality, Solingen steel manicure scissors. They're very sharp, sturdy, and come to a tiny point. Good-quality "stork" embroidery scissors also work well. When cutting off thread tails, use a trick Virginia Blakelock teaches and pull on the thread as you cut it. This stretches it slightly so the end hides inside the last bead. Also, never cut a thread immediately after a knot; pass it through a few beads before cutting, or the knot will come untied.

If you use clear nail polish as glue for your knots, apply a drop from the tip of your beading needle directly on the knot (another Virginia Blakelock trick). Never use the nail polish brush; the solvent could damage bead color or finish. I recommend G-S Hypo Cement for knots in elastic thread. In fact, those were the only knots I glued in these projects.

I recommend Barge Cement for making the a lining for a bracelet rather than E6000. Barge cement is usually available where leather is sold if your bead store doesn't carry it. It doesn't smell as horrible as E6000 and the smell eventually goes away, but the best reason for beaders to use Barge Cement is that it's more flexible and can be sewn through it in a pinch, unlike E6000.

## Crimping

I strung my beaded bead necklace on flexible beading wire, so I had to use crimps to attach the clasp to the ends. You can press a crimp flat with chain-nose pliers, but crimping pliers fold the crimp so it is less visible and slightly more secure. The jaws of crimping pliers have two stations. The one closer to the handles looks like a crescent moon, and the one at the end of the pliers is oval.

1. Separate the wires in the crimp with one hand and place the crimp in the crescent moon station of the pliers (photo 1). Press firmly. The goal is to have one wire on each side of the dent that this station puts into the crimp.

2. Turn the dented crimp sideways so the dent is centered between the pliers jaws in the oval station (photo 2).

3. Press down smoothly to fold the crimp at the dent (photo 3). For security, you may want to press the fold together with chain-nose pliers

## Knots

I've used only two knots in these projects: a surgeon's knot and pairs of half hitches. I tie the surgeon's knot in the reverse order from the method shown in recent books.

My method was taught me by my mother, who learned it from her brother when he was in medical school. It seems logical to me that the longer part of the knot will hold better if it curls around the shorter part. I learned the trick of tying two half hitches in the same place from Dori Jamieson. It's easier and safer than tying a double half hitch, which often tightens too soon. If I want really good hold from half hitches, I'll tie a pair of crossed half hitches.

### Surgeon's Knot

The surgeon's knot starts like a square knot.

1. Cross the left-hand end on top of the right-hand end, wrap it behind the right-hand cord, and bring it back to the front (lower green line). The right-hand tail (purple) now points left and the left-hand tail points right.

2. Bend the right-hand tail back toward the right and the left-hand tail back toward the left (middle of knot).

3. Cross the tail that's currently on the right (green), over the tail coming from the left (purple).

4. Wrap it behind that tail and pull it through the opening between the step 1 cross and the step 3 cross (this is a square knot).

5. To turn it into a surgeon's knot wrap behind, under, and through to the front again. The result is that the top of the knot curves partway down the sides of the first cross, which makes it more stable and less likely to twist out of the square when you tighten it.

6. Pull the tails in the directions they are pointing to tighten the knot.

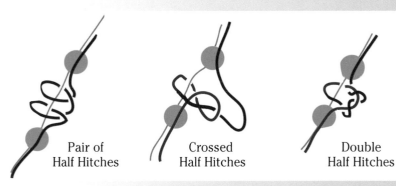

Pair of Half Hitches     Crossed Half Hitches     Double Half Hitches

## Half-Hitch Knot

1. For a plain half hitch, bring the needle through a bead. Then sew under the thread between this bead and the next bead. Tighten until a small loop remains.

2. Pass the needle through the loop, going over the thread that you previously sewed under (lower loop in pair of half hitches).

3. Repeat the process for a paired half hitch, at left, which is much more secure than a single half hitch.

4. For a crossed half hitch, center, repeat step 1 of the plain half hitch. Give the starting loop a half twist so its sides cross, then sew through it. Tighten carefully so it doesn't lock too soon.

5. Start a double half hitch, right, like a plain half hitch, but sew through the starting loop twice.

# Minaret Bracelet 'Square Stitch'

*Square stitch is rich with possibilities.*

As I neared completion of this book, I realized that I hadn't done anything with square stitch. My reason for omitting it had been that this simple stitch, which looks like loom weaving without the loom and is perfect for joining flat-sided beads to each other, didn't offer enough opportunities for variation from the expected. How wrong I was!

Decreasing is easy in square stitch. You just stop or start a row before the end of the previous row. Increasing offers a bit more challenge because a bead that extends beyond the edge can't be anchored securely to its neighbors, so it doesn't line up quite straight with the row it's on. A little embellishment at the ends of rows, however, conceals this slight imperfection.

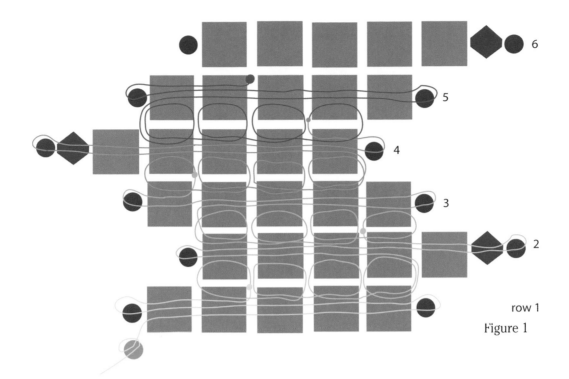

row 1

Figure 1

## Beads Used: Cubes • Rounds • Crystals

### SUPPLIES

30-40g Cube beads, 4mm
   (4C86, "oil-slick" luster black)
5-7g Round seed beads, size 11/0
   (11R86, "oil-slick" luster black)
24-26 Swarovski bicone crystals, 4mm
   (fuchsia)
Sterling silver 2-hole slide clasp
Beading needle, size 10
Beading thread, One-G, purple

### HOW-TO

The long edges of this square stitch band form a zigzag, which is accomplished by decreasing at one end of every 2 rows while increasing at the other end. After the increase bead on every even-numbered row, you add a crystal, then reverse increase and decrease sides on the next 2 rows.

## Weaving the Band

1. Thread a needle with 1½ to 2 yd. (1.4-1.8m) of beading thread and work with it single.

2. String a stop bead (use any small seed bead) to about 16" (41cm) from the end of the thread. You'll use the long tail to attach clasp.

3. String 5 cubes and an 11/0. Skip the seed bead and sew back through the cubes to the stop bead. String an 11/0 and sew back through the first 2 cubes (figure 1, yellow-green line to dot).

4. To begin square stitching row 2 to the first row, pick up a cube and sew through the second cube on row 1 away from the stop bead; position the new cube on top of the one you've sewn it to. Continue through the next row 1 cube (#3).

Pick up the second cube of row 2 and sew through the third cube of row 1 in the same direction; continue through cube #4.

Pick up cube #3 of row 2 and sew through cube #4 of row 1 in the original direction. Continue through cube #5.

Square stitch cube #4 of row 2 to cube #5 of row 1.

5. Sew through the 4 cubes of row 2 to the start. String an 11/0 and sew back through the 4 cubes.

6. Pick up the fifth cube, a crystal, and a seed bead. Skip the seed and sew back down the crystal and next 2 cubes (figure 1, medium yellow-green line to dot).

7. The increase changes edges on row 3. Square stitch a cube to cubes #4-1 of row 2.

With your needle exiting the first cube of row 2, sew back through the 4 cubes of row 3 to the start.

String a seed bead. Skip the seed and sew through 4 cubes of row 3. String the fifth cube and a seed bead. Skip the seed bead and sew back through fifth cube of row 3 (figure 1, light green line to dot).

8. To begin row 4, square stitch a cube to the first 4 cubes of row 3.

Sew back through the 4 cubes of row 4, pick up the fifth cube, a crystal, and a seed. Skip the seed and go back through the crystal and the 5 cubes of row 4. String a seed, skip it, and go through the end cube of row 4 (figure 1, medium green line to dot).

9. The direction changes again on row 5.

10. Square stitch 4 cubes to the first 4 cubes of row 4. Sew back through the 4 cubes of row 5, pick up a cube and a seed, skip the seed and sew back through the 5 cubes. Pick up a seed, skip it, and sew back through the first 2 cubes of row 5 (figure 1, dark green line to dot).

11. Work row 6 like row 2 and repeat steps 4-10 as many times as needed to make the bracelet the desired length minus the clasp. End with a step 10 for a symmetrical bracelet.

Minaret Bracelets

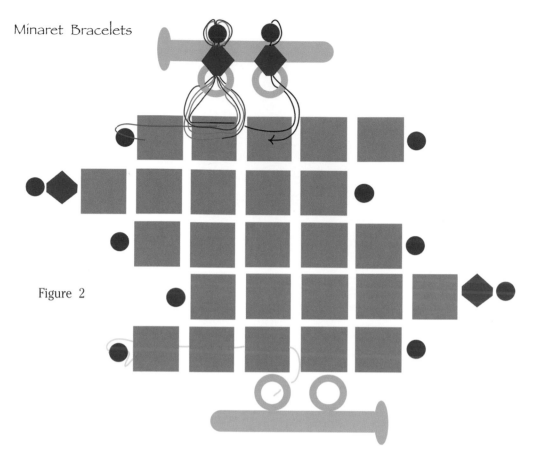

Figure 2

Beads Used:
Cubes • Rounds

## SUPPLIES
### LARGE Bead Bracelet
— page 10

MATERIALS:
12-15g Cube beads, 4mm, colorA
 (4C711F, brushed nickel-plated)
20g Cube beads, 4mm, color B
 (4C86, purple irid)
12-15g Cube beads, 4mm, color C
 (4C711, shiny nickel-plated)
7-10g Seed beads, size 8/0
 (8R1838 violet AB)
4 yd. Gossamer Floss (ribbon
 elastic), brown, gray, or purple
Short Big-Eye needle
G-S Hypo Cement

### SMALL Bead Bracelet
— page 11

MATERIALS:
20-25g Cube beads, 3mm
 (3C1058, purple-lined clear)
20-25g Cube beads, 3mm
 (3C2015, matte blue/purple)
10-15g Seed beads, size 8/0
 (8R627F, matte violet AB)
Beading thread, One-G, purple
Beading needle, size 10
24" (61cm) Gossamer Floss (ribbon elastic), brown or purple
Short Big-Eye needle
G-S Hypo Cement

## Ending and Adding Thread

1. Before ending a short thread, start a new thread three rows from the last. Sew through a few beads in the same direction that the thread is heading on the last row and tie a pair of half hitches around the thread between beads. Sew through 1-2 beads.

2. Step up to the second row from the end and sew through a bead or two in the opposite direction. Tie another knot, and go through a bead or two.

3. Step up to the last row and sew through it to bring the needle out the same bead as the short thread in the same direction. Resume beading.

4. When you have worked 4-5 rows, end the short thread in the first 3 new rows, following the same process you used to add the thread. Trim both tails.

## Attaching the Clasp

1. With the needle exiting the second bead from the end of the last row, sew up through the clasp loop closer to the stopper. String a crystal and a seed bead. Skip the seed and sew down the crystal.

2. Go through the second bead toward the near end. Come out the bead and sew up through the clasp loop. Go through the crystal and the seed bead then down the crystal and through bead #2 in the original direction (figure 2, light orange lines).

3. Reinforce the thread path on both sides of the bead again by repeating step 2 once or twice (figure 2, red lines).

4. Continue through the third bead (figure 2, dark red line). Repeat steps 1-3 to attach the second clasp loop to both sides of the third bead.

5. Then end the thread securely in the beadwork as described above.

6. Remove the stop bead from the starting tail and thread a needle on it. Sew through the end seed bead then the first 3 cubes.

7. Close the clasp so you are sure to attach it correctly. Make sure the crystals on this clasp part are on the same side of the bracelet as those on the first clasp part. (figure 2, light yellow-green line). Attach the clasp to the third and fourth beads of the starting row as in steps 1-5.

### HOW-TO
There are two differences between these bracelets: The 4mm bead version is woven entirely with Gossamer Floss; while the 3mm bracelet has only a short section woven with the elastic because the smaller bead holes would abrade the elastic too much if it was used throughout the bracelet. In addition, the bracelet made with 3mm cubes has 2 more beads per row than the 4mm cube bracelet.

# Working the Angles Bracelets
## 'Diagonal Peyote Stitch'

*Diagonal peyote stitch is used frequently by Russian beaders, but it's not familiar to most American beaders. It's the stitch used most often to make Russian leaves. I taught it to myself in 1998 when I had to figure out how a Russian piece had been made for an article I was editing, so I'm rather proud to have it in my stitch repertoire.*

*It's a handy stitch to know if you want a very flexible strip of peyote stitch; it's also a lot of fun once you get the hang of it. Cube beads work beautifully in this stitch.*

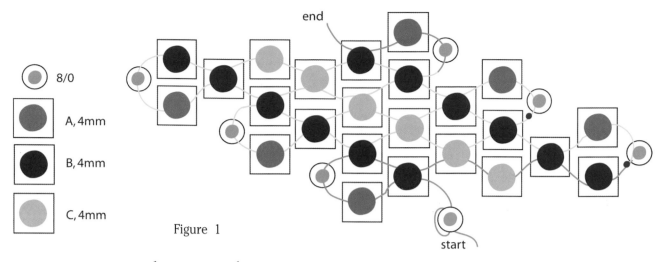

- 8/0
- A, 4mm
- B, 4mm
- C, 4mm

Figure 1

# Large-Bead Bracelet

1. Thread the Big-Eye needle on the Gossamer Floss close to the middle so you won't have to pull as much thread through the beads. Keep moving the needle along as you need more thread. Stretch the elastic slightly to tighten the beads after every 2-3 new beads.

Start by sewing through an 8/0 twice for a stop bead that you'll remove later. Leave a 6" (15cm) tail.

2. To start, pick up 1B, 1A, an 8/0, and 1B. Sew through the first B toward the stop bead. Then pick up 2C, and 2B (figure 1 to the first red dot).

3. The beading stitch pattern repeats from the first red dot to the second. Pick up an 8/0 and 1A for the end picot. Then sew through the first B toward the start. Pick up 1B and sew through the first C. Pick up 1C and sew through the B that was the fourth bead strung in step 2.

4. To make the starting edge picot, pick up 1B, 1A, an 8/0, and 1B and sew through the first B of this group toward the end picot edge. Tighten the thread and position the beads as shown in figure 1 with the A below the second B.

5. Continue working toward the end picot, adding 1C and sewing through the previous C, then adding 1B and sewing through the B (figure 1, second red dot).

6. Repeat steps 3-5 until the strip is long enough to fit around your wrist with about ½" (1.3cm) of ease. Stop after adding an

end picot and sewing back through the last B added (figure 1, top right).

7. Join the bracelet seamlessly as shown in figure 2. Bring the starting end around to meet the last row and position it so the 8/0 of the first end picot is above the last B on the final row. (Note: In figure 2, The lightened starting row at the bottom is repeated at the top of the figure.)

8. Do not remove the stop bead yet. Tighten the elastic on the first row to make sure it's snug.

9. Sew through the second B of row 1 (before the end picot) toward the start (see figure 2, red line, right to left).

Go through the last C added on the end, then the second C on row 1.

Sew through the B after the end row starting-edge picot. Then go through the first B strung at the start.

10. Remove the stop bead, tighten the starting thread again and put the needle on it. Then weave it into the last few rows of the bracelet, tying 2-3 half-hitch knots between beads. Go through 2 or 3 beads after the last knot.

11. Replace the needle on the ending thread. Make sure the last row is snug and end the thread in the beginning rows as in step 10.

12. Apply a dot of G-S Hypo Cement on each of the knots. Then squirt a little into the beads the two thread ends exit (this will keep the thread tails from popping out when you stretch the bracelet). When the glue is dry, cut off the excess thread.

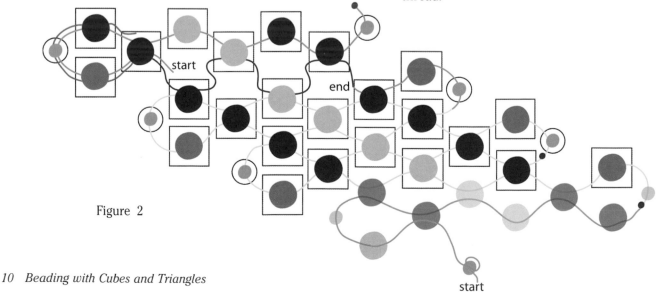

Figure 2

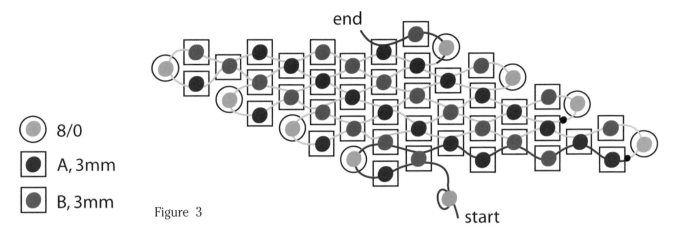

8/0

A, 3mm

B, 3mm

Figure 3

# Small-Bead Bracelet

1. Thread a beading needle with as long a length of beading thread as is comfortable for you. You will almost certainly have to add thread. Sew through an 8/0 twice for a stop bead that you'll remove later. Leave a 6" (15cm) tail.

2. To start, pick up 1B, 1A, an 8/0, and 1B. Sew through the first B toward the stop bead. Then pick up 2A, 2B, and 2A (figure 3, red line to the first black dot).

3. The beading stitch pattern repeats from the first black dot to the second. Pick up an 8/0 and 1B for the end picot. Then sew through the first A of the last pair toward the start. Pick up 1A and sew through the first B of the pair. Pick up 1B and sew through the first A of the first pair. Pick up 1 A and sew through the B that was the fourth bead strung in step 2 toward the 8/0.

4. To make the starting edge picot, pick up 1B, 1A, an 8/0, and 1B and sew through the first B of this group toward the end picot edge. Tighten the thread and position the beads as shown in figure 3 with the A below the second B.

5. Continue working toward the end picot, adding 1A and sewing through the previous A, 1B and sewing through the previous B, then adding 1A and sewing through the A added after the end picot (figure 3, second black dot).

6. Repeat steps 3-5 until the strip is about 1" (2.5cm) shorter than the desired length. (It should fit around your wrist with about ½" (1.3cm) of ease when completed.)

7. Weave and knot a 24" (61cm) length of Gossamer Floss threaded on a Big-Eye needle into the bracelet so that the working end exits the same bead as the beading thread. End the beading thread in the completed beadwork as in step 10 of the large-bead bracelet.

8. Weave the last inch (2.5cm) of the bracelet with Gossamer Floss so it will stretch over your hand. Tighten the elastic every few beads. Stop after adding an end picot and sewing back through the last A added (figure 3, top right).

Figure 4

9. Bring the starting end around to meet the last row and position it so the 8/0 of the end picot is above the last A added. In figure 4, the starting end being joined to the end is shaded lighter than the other beads.

10. Do not remove the stop bead yet. Tighten the thread on the first row to make sure it's snug.

11. Sew through the last A of row 1 (before the end picot) toward the start (see figure 4, red line, right to left).

Go through the last B added on the final row then the last B on row 1.

Sew through the first A on the final row, then the middle A of the starting row. Go through the first B of the last row, then the first B strung, sewing from the stop bead toward the starting edge picot.

12. Remove the stop bead, tighten the starting thread again and put a beading needle on it. Then weave it into the last few rows of the bracelet, tying 2-3 half-hitch knots between beads. Go through 2 to 3 beads after the last knot.

13. Make sure the elastic in the last row is snug and end the gossamer floss in the beginning rows as in step 10 of the large-bead bracelet (figure 4, the red line through the starting end picot).

14. Apply a dot of G-S Hypo Cement to each of the knots. Then squirt a little into the beads the two elastic thread ends exit (this will keep them from popping out). When the glue is dry, cut off the thread tails.

# Patchwork Bracelets
## 'Tubular Herringbone Stitch'

Make a beautiful textured bracelet by using two colors of cube beads or two sizes of triangle beads in a seamless tube.

We're really lucky that triangle and cube beads come in several sizes because the possibilities that occur when you combine sizes in a single piece are limitless. For a simple tubular herringbone bracelet, I decided to try a regular, offset alternation of two sizes.

The texture is wonderful and the project is very easy. The only slightly tricky part is grafting the end to the beginning for an invisible join.

Beads Used: Cubes • Triangles

## SUPPLIES
### CUBES Bead Bracelet

30-40g Cube beads, 4mm (4C613F matte gray)
20-25g Cube beads, 3mm (3C161 crystal AB)
Beading needle, size 10 or 12
Beading needle, size 10 or 12
Beading thread, One-G, white

### TRIANGLES Bead Bracelet

25-35g Triangle beads, size 8/0 (8T82F matte metallic blue iris)
15-20g Triangle beads, size 11/0 (11T612 matte slate blue)
Beading needle, size 10 or 12
Beading thread, One-G, medium blue

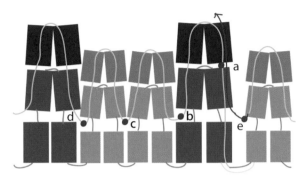

Figure 2

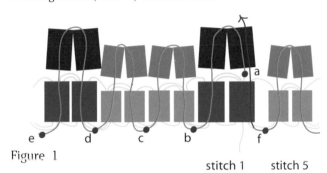

Figure 1

stitch 1    stitch 5

## Tubular Herringbone

1. Start by making a 10-bead ladder (see "Beaded Beads" on page 30) in the following pattern: 2 size 8/0s, 4 size 11/0s, 2 size 8/0s, 2 size 11/0s. Leave a 4-6" (10-15cm) thread tail and be extremely careful not to split a thread. You will remove the ladder beads to finish the bracelet.

Note: If you're making the bracelet with cube beads, ladder 2 4mm, 2 3mm, 2 4mm, and 2 3mm. You will have 4 herringbone stitches in the tube instead of 5. Work this bracelet like the triangle bracelet; soft tension is even more critical.

2. Do not reinforce the ladder before joining it into a ring as shown in "Beaded Beads."

3. Work a row of tubular herringbone following the established color and size bead pattern as follows:

a. With your needle exiting the first 8/0, pick up 2 size 8/0 beads and sew down the second 8/0 on the ladder (figure 1, a-b).

b. Sew up out of the first 11/0, pick up 2 size 11/0s and sew down the second 11/0 on the ladder (figure 1, b-c).

c. Sew up out of the third 11/0, pick up 2 size 11/0s and sew down the fourth 11/0 on the ladder (figure 1, c-d).

d. Sew up out of the first 8/0 in the next pair, pick up 2 size 8/0s and sew down the second 8/0 on the ladder (figure 1, d-e).

e. Repeat step b and you are finished adding beads for the first herringbone row (figure 1, e-f).

4. Notice that your needle is 2 rows of beads below the top of the tube. To step up so you can begin the next row, sew up the top 2 size 8/0s in the first column (figure 1, f to arrow).

5. Work a second herringbone row following the same color and size pattern. With your needle exiting the top of the first column of 8/0s, pick up 2 size 8/0s and sew down only the top 8/0 of the second column (figure 2, a-b).

Sew up the top 11/0 of the next column, pick up 2 size 11/0s and sew down the top bead of the fourth column (figure 2, b-c).

Sew up the top bead of the fifth column, pick up 2 matching beads, and sew down the top bead of the sixth column (figure 2, c-d).

Repeat around until you have added the last pair of 11/0s (figure 2, d-e).

6. Your needle is again 2 rows below the top, so step up through the top 2 beads of the first column (figure 2, e to arrow).

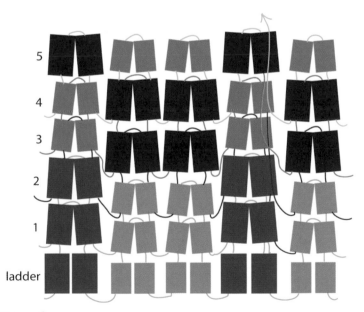

5
4
3
2
1
ladder

Figure 3

7. Now work 2 rows placing 11/0s over the 8/0s and 8/0s over the 11/0s (figure 3, rows 3 and 4).

8. Switch bead sizes after completing every 2 rows (figure 3, row 5). Continue in this manner until the tube will fit over the widest part of your hand with your thumb scrunched in under the middle of your palm.

9. You will have to end and add thread at least once. When the old thread is about 8" (20cm) long, stop after adding a pair of beads and sewing down the bead below.

a. Thread a needle with a new thread as long as you can use comfortably. Start 8-10 beads down from the top in the first column of the last stitch made (figure 4, brown line at bottom). Sew up about 3 beads and tie 2 half hitches around the thread between beads.

b. Sew up 2-3 more beads and knot again. Sew up 1-2 more beads and knot a third time, then exit the top bead at the beginning of the last stitch.

c. Sew down the second bead of the stitch and the bead below it. Then sew up the top bead of the next column to begin the next stitch with the new thread (figure 4, brown line at top).

d. End the old thread with 2-3 pairs of knots between beads as you continue sewing down the column you are in (figure 4, green line). End by going through a few beads. Then trim off the starting and ending tails.

new thread    old thread

Figure 4

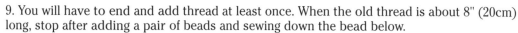
column #s    8    7    6    5    4    3    2    1    10    9

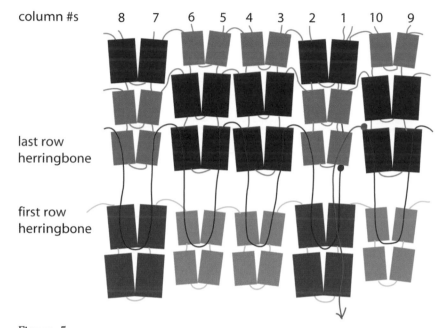

last row herringbone

first row herringbone

Figure 5

10. The last pair of rows must have 3 stitches made with 8/0s and 2 with 11/0s – the opposite of the first pair of rows. Repeat the thread path to reinforce the joining row. The working thread should be at least 15" (38cm) long. If it's too short, end it and add a new thread. Step up to exit the first bead of the first 11/0 stitch.

# Grafted Ends

1. Carefully unravel the starting ladder and remove the ladder beads. The beads on the first herringbone row will spread apart into stitches with pairs of different size beads. Thread a needle on the tail and reinforce the thread path of the first herringbone row. Then end the thread tail.

2. Bring the starting end around to meet the final end and match up the stitch columns (numbered at the top of figure 5).

3. With the working thread exiting the end 11/0 of the first stitch (figure 5, ruby dot), sew into the first 8/0 of the first stitch on the starting end. Sew out the second 8/0 and into the second 11/0 of the final end (photo 1).

4. Then sew out the first of the 4 size 8/0s on the end and into the first of the 4 size 11/0s of the start. Sew out the next 11/0 and into the second 8/0. Sew out the third 8/0 and into the third 11/0. Then sew out the fourth 11/0 and into the fourth 8/0.

5. Continue around (photo 2 and figure 5, ruby line) until you've sewn into the last 8/0 on the final end (figure 5, brown dot).

6. Sew out the first 11/0 of the final end and into the first 8/0 of the start. Continue through this column to end the thread with several knots between beads as described in step 9d above (figure 5, brown line).

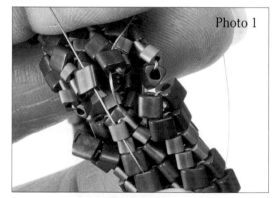
Photo 1

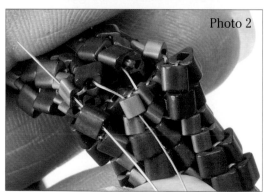
Photo 2

## Beads Used:
Cubes • Crystals • Rounds

## SUPPLIES

### GREEN Bracelet

25-30g Cube beads, 3mm
(3C940F matte olive green)
7-10g Seed beads, 11/0
(11R37 silver-lined green)
5g Seed beads, 14-15/0
(15R180 olive luster)
8-10 Swarovski bicone crystals, 6mm
(topaz)
48-60 Swarovski bicone crystals, 3mm
(topaz)

Beading thread, One-G (green)
Beading needles, size 10
Snap, size 1 or 2, or a shank button

### WHITE Bracelet
photo on page 17

25-30g Cube beads, 3mm
(3C21 silver-lined crystal)
7-10g Seed beads, 11/0
(Toho 11R29F matte silver-lined
crystal)
5g Seed beads, 14-15/0
(15R611 dark matte gray)
8-10 Swarovski bicone crystals, 6mm
(jet)
48-60 Swarovski bicone crystals, 3mm
(Black diamond)

Beading thread, (K-O light gray)
Beading needles, size 10
Snap, size 1 or 2, or a shank button

# Window Bracelets
## 'Peyote Stitch'

*I love the effect of openings in beadwork. It would have been very easy to work this bracelet without windows, but I'd have lost at least half the sparkle and half the fun.*

*In order to center the windows and the points on the bracelet ends, it must be worked in flat, odd-count peyote stitch, which means that you'll have an easy turn to the next row on one edge and a hard turn on the other.*

*The hard and easy edges will alternate after every window.*

An eight-window bracelet is 6½" (16.5cm) long and each additional window adds ¾" (2cm).

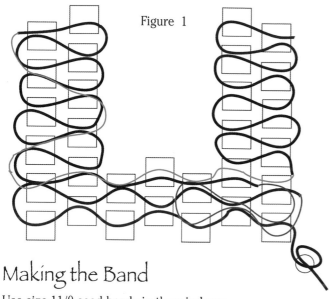

Figure 1

## Making the Band

Use size 11/0 seed beads in the windows.

1. Thread a needle with as long a thread as is comfortable and secure a stop bead about 18-20" (45-51cm) from the end.

2. String 7 cubes for rows 1 and 2 and peyote stitch a total of 4 rows (figure 1). Note that the first hard turn comes at the end of row 3 and is on the right (red line). See page 18 for "Flat Odd-Count Peyote Stitch".

3. Work the easy turn on the left at the end of row 4 then 8 rows of 2 beads along the left-hand edge.

After adding the fourth bead on the inner edge, zigzag down the edge and across the last full row (figure 1, blue line) to exit the right-hand edge bead.

4. Work 8 rows of 2 beads on this edge.

5. With the needle exiting the edge bead, go diagonally down through 2 beads to exit the middle bead on the inner side. Pick up an 11/0 seed bead, a 6mm crystal, and another 11/0 and sew into the matching bead on the inner edge of the left-hand side. Sew diagonally up to exit the edge. Then come back through the edge bead below and the same inner edge bead (figure 2, black line to green line).

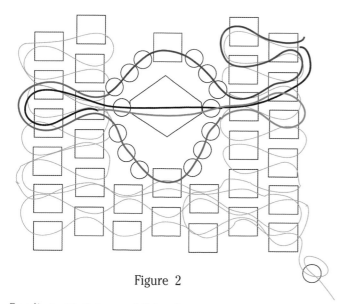

Figure 2

6. Reinforce the crystal and seed beads by sewing through them again and into the same inner edge bead on the right. Make the same looping motion to exit this bead again on the inside of the window (figure 2, green line).

7. String 3 seed beads and go through the middle bead on the bottom of the window. Then string 3 more seeds and enter the middle bead on the left-hand side of the window. Loop down then up to come out the same bead (figure 2, blue line to violet line).

8. String 3 seeds, a cube, and 3 seeds and sew into the middle bead on the right-hand side of the window. Then zigzag upward through the right-hand edge to exit the same bead from which you began in step 5 (figure 2, violet line).

9. Pick up a bead and work peyote stitch across to the other edge, adding 4 beads. The cube strung between the seed beads is the middle bead of the row below (figure 3, lower black line). Work a hard turn on the left-hand edge this time (figure 3, red to gray line) and peyote back across to the right. Work an easy turn and peyote back to the left (figure 3, gray line).

Work a hard turn (figure 3, orange line) and peyote across to the right (figure 3, dark blue line). Notice that the middle of this section is 3 beads tall.

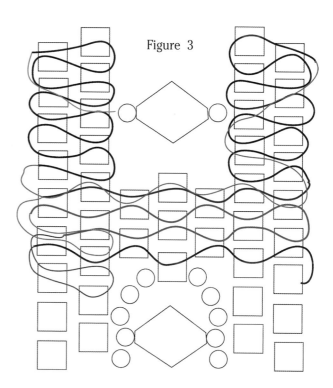

Figure 3

10. Work 8 rows of 2 beads on the right (figure 3, black line), then zigzag down to the last full row and across to the left (figure 3, medium blue line) to work eight 2-bead rows on the left. Sew diagonally down to the middle bead on the inside edge (figure 3, light blue line) and fill the window as in steps 5-8. Notice that this time you start on the left.

11. Then repeat step 9 to work the rows above the window. This time the hard turns will be on the right.

12. Repeat steps 4-11 until the bracelet is about ½" (1.3cm) short of the desired length and you've completed a step 11. Leave the thread in place.

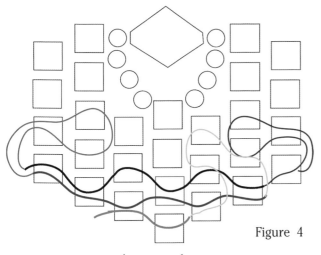

Figure 4

## Tapering the Ends

1. Go back to the starting edge of the bracelet and remove the stop bead. Thread a needle on the long tail. Your needle is exiting the bottom right-hand bead. Work a hard turn as shown by the red line on figure 4 so that your needle is now exiting the inner side of the same bead.

2. Peyote across, adding 3 cubes. Then work the hard turn shown by the orange line on the left-hand side of figure 4 so that you are heading to the right. Add 2 beads on this row (figure 4, dark blue line).

3. Work the turn shown by the yellow line to position your needle heading left through the last bead added, and add 1 bead (figure 4, light blue line).

4a. Weave the tail into the beadwork. If you are clasping your bracelet with a snap, sew it to the wrong side of the pointed end so that its outer edge is even with the next-to-last center cube bead (figure 4, green outline).

4b. If you are clasping your bracelet with a button and loop, weave the thread into the beadwork so it exits either side of the next-to-last center cube bead (figure 4, green outline). Sew the button on top of this bead, going through the bead and the button's shank at least 5 times. Then end the thread by weaving it into the beadwork.

5. Return to the thread at the other end of the bracelet and finish it with a matching taper.

6a. If using a snap, sew it to the right side of the bracelet positioned identically to the first part.

6b. If you are using a button, weave the thread into the beadwork, then bring it out through the tip bead. String enough 11/0 seed beads to make a loop that will fit over the button with a tiny bit of ease. Reinforce the loop by sewing through it at least 3-4 times. Then end the thread in the beadwork.

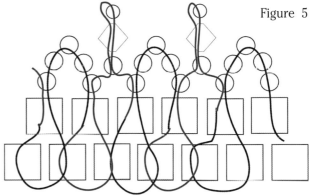

Figure 5

## Edging the Bracelet

1. If you are left with a long working thread, weave it through the beadwork to exit the end edge bead on either edge. If the working thread is short or frayed, end it and add a new thread.

2. Pick up 5 size 11/0 seed beads and sew into the next edge bead (figure 5, black line on right).

3. Sew diagonally down one bead on the next row from the edge. Come out the adjacent bead and then the edge bead you entered.

4. Sew through the last seed bead, string 1 seed, a 3mm crystal, and a 15/0 seed. Skip the 15/0 and sew back down the crystal and seed bead. Pick up 1 seed and sew into the third edge bead (figure 5, red line on right).

5. Loop through the beads on the two edge rows as in step 3 and exit the same cube you entered and the last seed added.

6. Pick up 4 more seeds and sew into the fourth cube (figure 5, second black line).

7. Repeat from step 3. You will end with a 5-seed bead loop that enters the last edge bead on this side.

8. End the thread securely. Then add a new thread at one end of the other edge and repeat the edging pattern.

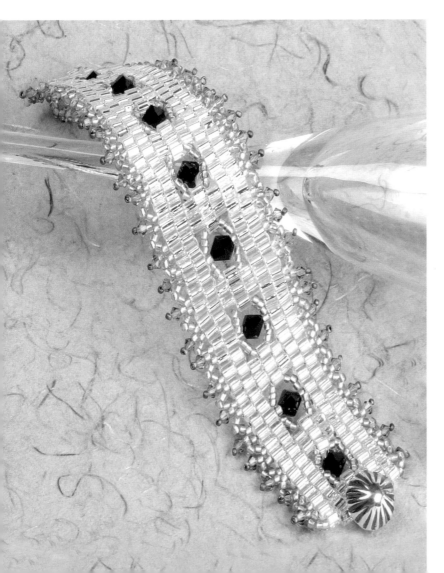

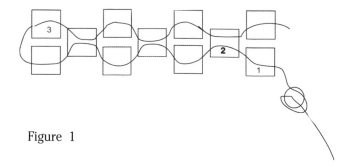

Figure 1

## Flat Odd-Count 'Peyote Stitch'

1. Sew a stop bead, a small waste bead, near the end of the thread by passing the needle through it twice. Be careful not to split the thread so you can remove the stop bead easily later (figure 1).

2. Pick up an odd number of beads for the first 2 rows. The first and last bead will be on row 1 and the beads between alternate row 2 and row 1.

3. Pick up the first bead for row 3 (Note: count peyote rows on the diagonal) and sew back through the next-to-last bead, a row 2 bead, toward the stop bead.

4. Pick up the next row 3 bead, skip a bead (row 1), and sew through the next bead (row 2). The row 3 beads are positioned above the row 1 beads.

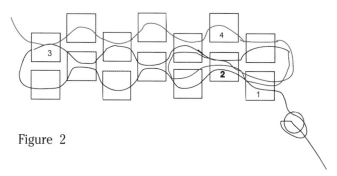

Figure 2

5. When you pick up the last row 3 bead, there is no place to anchor it. To fasten it above the first bead (row 1), you must work the "hard turn" as follows:

a. Sew through the first 3 beads strung in that order (figure 2, red line).

b. Turn so the needle points toward the near edge and sew through the next-to-last row 3 bead (figure 2, fuchsia line).

c. Angle diagonally down and go through the second bead strung then the first bead strung (figure 2, fuchsia line continued).

d. Now turn the needle to point toward the other edge and sew through the last row 3 bead added.

6. Pick up the first row 4 bead and go through the next row 3 bead. Continue in this manner across the row. You will end coming out the edge row 3 bead (figure 2, green line).

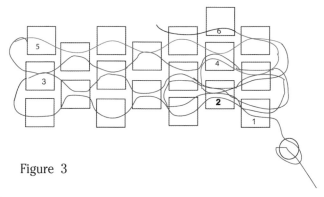

Figure 3

7. On this edge (the one opposite the stop bead), you can work an easy turn. Pick up the first row 5 bead. Position it above the row 3 bead you just exited and go through the last row 4 bead added (figure 3, green line).

8. Pick up a row 5 bead before sewing through each row 4 bead.

9. You will have to work a modified hard turn at the end of this row to attach the last row 5 bead:

a. Sew through the edge bead toward the other edge and continue diagonally down through 1 more bead (figure 3, fuchsia line).

b. Turn and sew through the bead above the one you just went through toward the near edge. Continue diagonally down to come out the edge bead you went through in step a (figure 3, blue line).

c. Now go through the new edge bead above it toward the far edge (figure 3, blue line) and add the row 6 beads (black line), repeating from step 6.

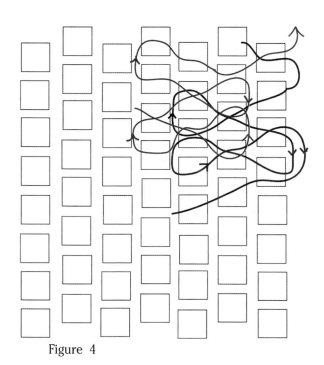

Figure 4

## Ending and Adding Thread

In peyote stitch, I end and add threads by weaving them through the beads on crossing diagonals with at least three crosses (figure 4). Add a new thread (red) before ending the old one (black) so that you are certain to bring the new thread out the same bead in the same direction as the old thread.

# Glitzy Button Bracelet
## 'Variation of Netting'

*At a bead store, I couldn't resist a short strand of vintage Swarovski, flat, sew-on crystals. So I didn't. I knew they'd be perfect for the tops of buttons made with 4mm cube beads. If you can't find the flat crystals, 6mm bicones or rounds will also work; they'll just stick up a bit more.*

*I also made my own hook clasp with gold-filled or sterling silver wire because a commercial clasp would have added too much length to the bracelet and would have created a large visible space between buttons. The clasp directions included below are adapted from a clasp taught me by Trudy Edlebeck.*

**Beads Used:** Cubes • Rounds • Crystals

## SUPPLIES

20-25g Cube beads,
    4mm (matte metallic purple/bronze 4C615; matte raku antique gold 4C513F; metallic green-gold – Miyuki)
10g Round seed beads,
    size 8/0 (matte burgundy/purple 8R104; matte heavy luster topaz 8R177F; matte, silver-lined, luster topaz)
8-10 Swarovski crystals, 6mm, flat rounds, bicone, or round (vintage sapphire champagne; foil-backed vitral)
Beading thread One-G, light blue or purple; light brown
Beading needles, sizes 10 and 12
Small clasp or make your own with 4" (10cm) sterling silver or gold-filled wire, 20- or 22-gauge, half-hard, round
If making clasp: beading pliers
    (chain-nose, flat-nose, round-nose) and flush cutter

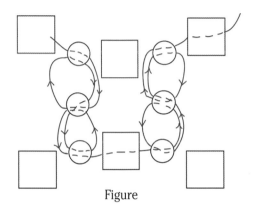

Figure

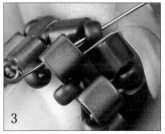

## How to Make a Button

Each button is ⅞" (2.2cm) long. Subtract the length of your clasp from the desired length of the bracelet to determine the number of buttons you'll need. The bracelet should fit with only a little ease. Choose longer cubes for the base ring, medium-length cubes for the top, and short cubes for the underside.

1. With a 1-yd. (.9m) thread and a size 10 needle, string 8 long cubes alternated with 8 fat size 8/0 seed beads. Go through all 16 beads again and tie them into a firm ring with 1 or 2 surgeon's knots.

2. Sew through 1-2 beads to exit an 8/0. String a medium cube, 8/0, and a medium cube and sew through the next 8/0 on the ring. Sew back up the second cube (photo 1).

Note: for the antique gold bracelet, I also strung an 8/0 before the first cube and after the second then sewed up the last 8/0 and second cube – as on the button for the "Octagon Bracelet."

3. String an 8/0 and a cube (plus an 8/0 for the antique gold bracelet). Sew through the third 8/0 on the ring and back up the last (8/0 and) cube.

4. Repeat step 3 until you have added the eighth cube and sewn back up it. String an 8/0 and sew down the first cube (photo 2).

5. Sew through the 8/0 on the ring from which you began and go back up the first cube (photo 3) then the first top 8/0.

6. Sew through all 8 of the top 8/0s twice to pull the top ring together snugly. If necessary, secure it with 2 pairs of half hitches.

7. Coming out any of the top 8/0s, string a crystal. Skip 3 8/0s and sew through the fourth. Sew back through the crystal, then the 8/0 from which you started in this step (photo 4). Tighten the thread, being careful not to pull it against the edge of the crystal's hole. Repeat the thread path several times to reinforce the crystal.

8. Sew down through beads to exit any cube on the starting ring. Turn the button over so the bottom is up.

9. To reinforce the button shape, string 3 short cubes and sew through the cube on the starting ring directly opposite the one from which you started. Sew back through the 3 cubes and through the starting cube (photo 5). Repeat the thread path.

10. Sew through 2 cubes on the bar and pick up a slightly shorter or a short and irregular cube. Sew through the middle cube on the bar in the same direction as before. Push the short cube under the middle cube (photo 6) and tighten the thread.

11. With the thread exiting the middle cube on the bar, pick up 1 short cube and sew through the ring cube midway between the ones to which the bar is attached. Sew back through the new cube and the middle bar cube in the original direction, centering the new cube against it (photo 7).

12. Attach another short cube to the middle ring cube on the other side of the bar and come back through the middle bar cube. You will have to force the side cubes into position; if they are too long, they won't fit. Check to make sure the thread isn't wrapped around the corner of a cube, that it holds the side cubes firmly. Reinforce the bar (photo 8).

13. Sew through beads on the ring to exit an 8/0 adjacent to the line of the hole through the crystal.

14. Weave and knot the starting thread tail securely into all the buttons but one. On this button, leave a 10-12" (25-30cm) starting tail and position it in an 8/0 adjacent to the other end of the crystal's hole.

## Joining the Buttons

1. Start with the button that has two thread tails. Using the longer thread, pick up an 8/0 and square stitch it to the 8/0 the thread exits by sewing through it in the original direction (photo 9 and figure, p. 20). Then go through the new 8/0 again. Reinforce the thread path.

2. Pick up a second button and square stitch the new 8/0 to the appropriate 8/0 next to the crystal's hole on the end opposite the second button's thread tail (photo 10).

3. Reinforce the thread path between these 3 beads. Then sew through the cube on either button to the 8/0 on the other side of the crystal's hole. Square stitch an 8/0 to this bead and attach it to the matching 8/0 on the other button (photo 11). Reinforce the thread path and end the thread in either button with several pairs of half hitches between beads.

4. Thread the thread tail on button #2 on a needle and attach this button to button #3 in the same manner. Repeat the process to join all the buttons.

5. Use the thread tail on the last button to sew one part of the handmade clasp directly to the pair of 8/0s on each side of the crystal's hole (photo 12). Reinforce the attachment with several thread passes. Then end the thread securely in the button.

6. Use the long starting tail on the first button to attach the other clasp part the same way.

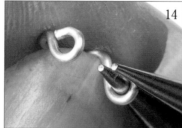

## Making a Short Loop Clasp

1. Cut a 1¼" (3.1cm) piece of wire for the loop part of the clasp.

2. Using the widest part of your round-nose pliers, bend the center into a shallow arc slightly wider than a cube bead's length.

3. Holding the arc in flat-nose pliers, bend the wire ends out of the plane of the arc at a right angle (photo 13).

4. Trim the ends flush and slightly longer than ¼" (6-7mm).

5. Roll each end into a small, centered loop that meets the arc wire snugly (photo 14).

6. For the hook part, bend the center of a 2½" (6.4cm) wire

into a U shape around the medium width of your round-nose pliers.

7. Grasp the bent part of the wire at about the middle of the round-nose pliers and bend it over to form a hook (photo 15).

8. Using flat-nose pliers, hold the double wire slightly beyond the hook tip and bend the wire tails away from the hook at a right angle (photo 16).

9. Hold each wire steady with a pair of pliers and bend the wire before the right-angle bend outward slightly until the tails are aligned with the 8/0s on each side of a cube bead (photo 17).

10. Trim the tails as in step 4 and roll each up into a small, snug loop. Then bend the loops so they are parallel to each other and the desired distance apart (photo 18).

# Egyptian Wave Bracelet 'Peyote Stitch'

*Although this bracelet looks extremely complicated, it isn't. It's made with odd-count flat peyote stitch and triangle beads in two sizes. The wonderful effect comes from the fact that the large beads spread the beadwork and the small beads contract it.*

*To get the best results, work with a firm tension and take advantage of size variation in your triangle beads. When you are increasing the number of size 8/0 beads across a row, the spaces the new 8/0s fit into are narrow, so choose short 8/0s for them. Use full-size 8/0s above previous 8/0s.*

*You'll have the opposite problem when you are decreasing the number of 8/0s and increasing the number of 11/0s: the spaces are wide where the new 11/0s go. So choose the longest 11/0s you can find to fill them. Use standard size 11/0s above previous 11/0s.*

# Beads Used: Triangles

## SUPPLIES

50g Triangle beads, size 8/0 (8T83 metallic bronze iris)
30g Triangle beads, size 11/0 (11T223 new bronze)
24-32 Round seed beads, size 8/0 (8R83 or a color that blends; these beads won't show)
2 to 2½" (5-6.4cm) Fine chain (I used gold-filled figure-8)
2 Gold-tone or gold-filled small magnetic clasps
Beading thread dark brown One-G or smoke Fireline
Beading needles, size 10
Optional:
    Needle file set to smooth rough metal on clasp loops
    or 4 split rings, 4mm, gold-filled

## HOW-TO

My 6¼" (15.9cm) bracelet has 12 complete size 8/0 diamonds. A 7" (17.8) bracelet will need 13 and a 7½" (19cm) bracelet will need 14. As you work, fit the bracelet around your wrist without stretching it to determine the number of diamonds needed for a comfortable fit with very little ease.

1. Use the longest thread that is comfortable. Too long a thread will tangle. Sew a stop bead 12-18" (30-46cm) from the end of the thread and string the following pattern for rows 1 and 2: 7 size 11/0 triangles, 1 size 8/0 triangle, and 7 size 11/0 triangles. For a refresher on odd-count flat peyote and ending and adding thread, see "Peyote Window Bracelet" on pages 15 - 18.

2. Follow the chart for this bracelet, starting with row 3. Odd-numbered rows are labeled on the right-hand side of the chart. Choose beads that will fit into the spaces available for them.

3. Photo 1 shows the next-to-last bead on row 7. Notice that it is narrower than the 8/0s in the middle of the band. Also notice how narrow the 8/0 added to its left on the row below is. The goal is to be able to fit the new beads in so they lie straight and flat against the bead below.

Don't worry about turning the triangles so the flat side is up; some will show an angle and others a side.

4. Photo 2 shows the last bead, an 8/0 being added on row 9 and the beginning of the hard turn to attach it. Pick up the edge bead and sew through the edge bead below it and diagonally down through the next bead.

5. Sew back toward the edge through the bead above and the edge bead you went into before (photo 3). Now sew through the new edge bead to begin row 10.

6. On row 10, add 7 size 8/0 beads, making sure to use standard-size beads (photo 4). The goal is to expand the diamond to its widest on this row. Notice that at this point the diamond lies flat.

7. The first and last beads on row 11 are size 11/0 triangles. Choose the longest you can find so the step to a shorter bead is minimized on the edges (photo 5).

8. On row 16, you add only one size 8/0 in the center space on the row. In photo 6, notice that although I am picking the longest 11/0s

I can, they are still shorter than the spaces I am filling. To compensate, pull the thread tight and maintain a firm tension. This causes the beadwork to contract and the 8/0 diamond to pop outward.

9. Photo 7 shows the middle stitch on row 20, the first 8/0 of the next diamond. Notice that the 11/0s fit together without gaps and the diamond cups deeply as a result of the snug tension.

10. Work through row 27. Then work rows 10 through 27 until you have the number of 8/0 diamonds needed. Finish the last diamond by working rows 10 through 18, a 7-bead row of 11/0s. Weave the thread into the bracelet to secure the tension. If you have at least 24" (61cm), you can use it to attach the clasp at this end. If not, end and cut off the thread.

11. Return to the starting end of the bracelet and remove the stop bead. Thread a needle on the tail. Turn (photo 8) and work a final row of 7 size 11/0 beads, then end the thread securely.

## Adding the Clasp

To make the bracelet look continuous, I've hidden two magnetic clasps on the inside set so that the magnets reach just shy of the end rows. I've added a safety chain to ensure that I don't lose my bracelet.

1. Some magnetic clasps have rough metal on the edges of the loops that will cut your thread. Either file them smooth or attach a small split ring, not a jump ring, to the loop on each clasp part. Keep the two clasps closed so you don't mix up the parts. Two parts with the same polarity won't work.

2. Work the long thread or a new thread to the middle of the first inside rib and sew through the fourth bead from the end on the inside (photo 9).

3. Since I did not use split rings on my clasp parts, 3 size 8/0 round seed beads extended the magnet to the desired length. (If you use a 4mm split ring, 2 thin seed beads will probably be right.) For the first clasp, string the desired number of seed beads, the clasp (leave the other part of the clasp stuck to it), and the same number of seed beads. Sew through the same triangle in the same direction and repeat the thread path 3-4 more times.

4. Work the thread through the beadwork to the matching bead at the other end of the first inside rib.

5. String the desired number of seed beads the end link of the safety chain, the other clasp, and the same number of seed beads. Sew back through the triangle bead and reinforce the attachment with 3-4 more thread passes (photo 10). Then weave the thread into the beadwork to end it securely.

6. Attach a new thread at the other end of the bracelet in the same position as the first clasp and repeat step 3 to attach the other part of that clasp.

7. Work the thread through the beads to the matching bead for the second clasp, the one with the chain, and repeat step 5 to attach the other end link of the chain and the other clasp part (photo 11).

# Pleated Bracelet
## 'Peyote Stitch'

*Like the Egyptian Wave Bracelet, this bracelet achieves its pleated look from the use of two sizes of triangle beads worked in odd-count flat peyote. The triangles formed with the large beads puff outward; while those formed with the smaller beads recede.*

*I added two rows of triangle bead edging to each of the triangles. In the case of the triangles made with size 8/0 beads, the edging adds a graceful curve that smooths an ugly straight edge and hides thread and bead holes. The edging is necessary on the small bead triangles, not only to conceal the thread and bead holes, but also to spread these triangles so that both long edges of the bracelet are about the same length. Without this edging, the bracelet looks more like a doll's skirt than a woman's bracelet.*

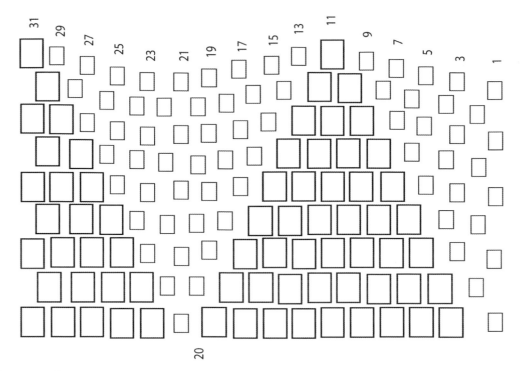

## Beads Used: Triangles

### SUPPLIES

30-40g Triangle beads, 8/0 (8T82 metallic blue iris)
20-30g Triangle beads, 11/0 (11T288 colonial blue-lined crystal)
Beading needle, size 10
Thread: medium blue One-G or Fireline
Sterling silver slide clasp, 4-loop

### HOW-TO

My bracelet has eight complete large-bead triangles and is 6¾" (17cm) around on the small bead edge and 7¼" (18.4cm) around on the large bead edge. Each large-bead triangle repeat adds about ⅞" (2.2cm). Wear the bracelet with the small bead edge at your wrist.

For a refresher on odd-count flat peyote and ending and adding thread, see "Peyote Window Bracelet" on pages 15 - 18.

## Weaving the Band

1. Start the bracelet by sewing a stop bead about 18-24" (46-61cm) from the end of the thread (you'll use the tail to add the clasp). String 9 size 11/0 triangle beads for rows 1 and 2 (starting on the left-hand edge of the chart; odd numbered rows are numbered on the right-hand side, where they begin).

2. For row 3, add 4 size 11/0 triangles and end with one 8/0.

3. As you continue beading, pick narrow 8/0s to fit in the spaces between the 11/0s. You want the new large beads to spread the beadwork but still fit into their spaces. On the return row, place a normal-size 8/0 above a short 8/0. This will spread the beadwork further. Take a look at the process photos in "Egyptian Wave Bracelet" to see how this process works.

Note: Don't worry about turning the triangles so the flat side is out. Some will present only an angle and others will show a side on the surface of the beadwork. Let them fall as they will.

4. On row 13, you begin contracting the beadwork by adding 11/0s to create the first complete small bead triangle. As with the "Egyptian Wave Bracelet," pick long 11/0s to fit over 8/0s.

Then use normal-size 11/0s on subsequent rows. Keep the tension snug so the beads fit firmly together. The small bead triangle will pull to the inside and the large bead triangle will puff outward.

5. Work to row 20. Then repeat rows 1-20 for the number of multiples needed. End the bracelet with row 21, which is the same as row 1. Secure the last row by weaving the thread through the beadwork. If it is short, cut it off; if it is long, weave it back out the last edge 11/0 and leave it in place.

Figure 1

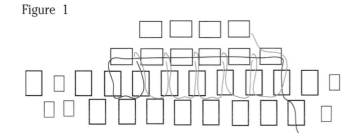

## Edging the Large Triangles

1. Weave a new 1 to 1½ yd. (.9-1.4m) thread into the beadwork to exit the second edge bead of the first 8/0 triangle (figure 1, dark brown line on right).

2. String 6 size 8/0 triangles and sew down the next-to-last edge bead of the first large triangle (#8). Sew up and out the next edge bead back (#7 – figure 1, dark brown line on left).

3. To couch the strand of beads to the edge, sew around the thread between the last 2 beads and sew down the same edge bead you exited (#7 – figure 1, yellow line on left).

4. Sew up edge bead #6 and couch between the fifth and fourth beads on the strand. Sew back down #6 and up #5.

5. When you have couched between the first and second strand beads and gone down edge bead #3, come back up #2 and sew through the first bead of the strand (figure 1, the end of the yellow line).

Figure 2

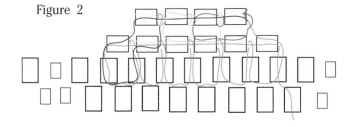

6. String 4 size 8/0 triangles, sew through the sixth bead on the first edging row, then sew down edge bead #8 and up #7. Sew left to right through the fifth bead of edging row 1 (figure 2, brown line).

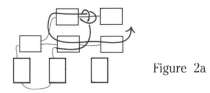

Figure 2a

7. To attach the second edging row firmly to the first, couch between beads with half-hitch knots as shown in figure 2a:

a. Bring the thread over the front of the thread between beads 3 and 4 of row 2. Then go behind the thread and sew to the front below it (figure 2a, dark red to bright red line).

b. Do not pull the loop tight yet. Sew through it from right to left and go through bead #4 to the left. Tighten the knot.

c. Sew through the bead below in the first row and continue through the next bead (figure 2a, bright red line).

8. Repeat steps 7a-c twice more (figure 2, yellow and green lines). After sewing through the second bead of row 2, go through the third and second beads of row 1 (figure 2, orange line). Then sew into the first bead of row 2 (figure 2, dark green line).

9. Sew through the 4 beads of row 2 and the last bead of row 1. Then travel though the beads along the edge of the bracelet as shown in figure 3 so you can exit the second edge bead of the next large triangle. Repeat the above steps to edge it.

10. Edge all the large triangles. Then end the thread securely in the beadwork.

Figure 3

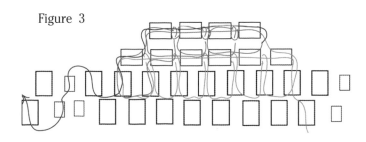

Figure 4

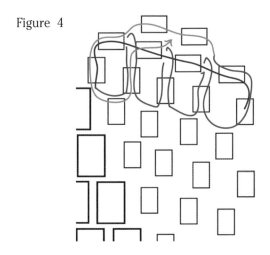

# Edging the Small Triangles

The bracelet begins and ends with a half-width small triangle. The edging process is similar to that for the large triangles and the whole small triangles, but the bead counts are different.

1. With the thread exiting the edge bead of the end small half-triangle, String 4 size 11/0 triangle beads and sew down the last 11/0 edge bead of the half triangle (#5). Sew back up #4 and couch between the third and fourth beads of edging row 1 (figure 4, dark blue line).

2. Repeat the couching process between the edging beads as in steps 1-5 of the large triangles. End by sewing up the edge bead of the triangle and through the first bead of edging row 1 (figure 4, medium blue line).

3. String 2 size 11/0 triangles and sew through the last bead of row 1, down the last edge triangle, up the next-to-last, and through the third bead of edging row 1 (figure 4, light blue line).

Figure 5

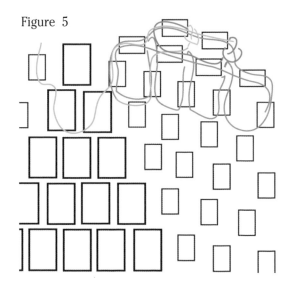

Figure 7

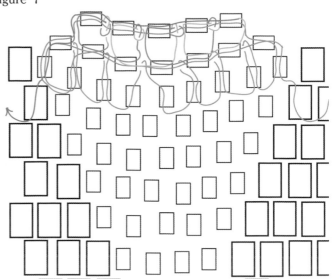

4. As shown in figure 2a and step 7 of the large triangle, tie a half-hitch couching stitch between the 2 beads of row 2 (figure 5, light green line). Then go right to left through the last bead of row 2 and left to right through the third bead of row 1. Continue through the second bead and knot around the thread at the beginning of row 2 (figure 5, green line).

5. Sew right to left through both beads of row 2 and the last bead of row 1. To reposition your needle so you can edge the first complete small triangle, continue down the edge bead of the half triangle, diagonally down the 8/0 bead below, up the 8/0 next to it, and diagonally up the first edge bead of the next 11/0 triangle (figure 5, yellow line).

10. Knot around the thread between the last 2 row 2 beads as shown in figure 2a and continue in this manner to secure the row 2 beads to the row 1 beads (figure 7, orange and yellow lines).

11. After the last knot go through the second row 1 bead toward the right, then go right to left through all the row 2 beads. Follow the green line on the left to get the next size 11/0 triangle (figure 7).

12. When you have edged the last half triangle like the first, end the thread securely in the beadwork.

Figure 6

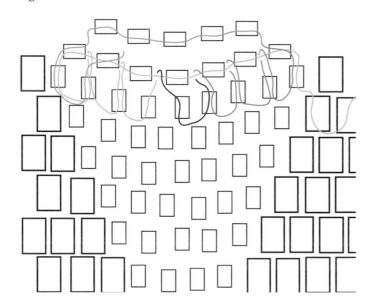

6. For row 1 of a complete small triangle, string 7 size 11/0 triangle beads and sew down the last bead on the edge of the triangle (#9). Sew up the next bead and make two normal couching stitches (figure 6, yellow line).

7. After sewing around the thread between the fifth and fourth beads of row 1, sew down bead #5 of the triangle, rather than the bead you exited (figure 6, dark red line).

8. Sew up bead #4 and make 3 more normal couching stitches. Then sew up the first triangle bead and go through the first row 1 edging bead (figure 6, orange line).

9. String 5 size 11/0 triangle beads for the second edging row and sew right to left through the last bead of the first row. Sew down then up the last 2 edge beads and go left to right through the next-to-last row 1 bead (figure 6, blue line).

## Attaching the Clasp

1. Either attach a new 18-24" (46-61cm) thread at one end of the band or use a long enough extant thread. The thread needs to be exiting the end bead and pointing toward the other edge.

2. Attach the inner part of the sliding clasp first with the stopper end on the large triangle edge so it will open upward (toward the large triangles).

3. Sew through the first "down" size 11/0 triangle. Place the clasp on the inner side of the band with the first loop against this "down" bead and sew through the clasp loop, then the "down" bead. Photo 1 shows this process on the final clasp loop.

4. Sew through the clasp loop again and go back through the down bead (photo 2).

5. Repeat this process, going back and forth through the down bead, to make 2-3 stitches around each side of the clasp loop. Then sew through the next 2 beads, exiting the second "down" bead and repeat to attach each loop to a down bead.

6. Close the clasp to make sure that you start attaching it to the other end correctly. As soon as you've made the first stitch, you can separate the clasp so it's easier to attach.

# Necklace of Beaded Beads
# 'Brick Stitch'

*How do you make a beaded round bead with non-round beads? That was an interesting puzzle, but the answer turns out to be pretty straightforward. Create a ring of diamond shapes that fits the circumference of a round wooden bead. Then connect the ends of the diamonds with two rounds of peyote stitch, using round seed beads and lace the sides of the diamonds together with more seed beads. The result is far prettier than I had expected.*

*Triangle beads present flat sides that catch the light and sparkle brilliantly. Add to that the interplay of round and rectangular shapes and the contrast between horizontal bands of seed beads and the vertical orientation of triangle beads, and the result is a very snazzy bead, indeed.*

*To give the necklace a sophisticated, graduated design, I used five sizes of wooden beads. I added a look of complexity without its reality by alternating beads in two contrasting color palettes – that were unified by the repetition of one color between the palettes – and by varying the patterns within each bead size.*

## HOW-TO

I've included two pattern charts for the 20mm beads and three charts for the 16 and 14mm beads; make two beads in each pattern in each size. There are 4 charts for the 10mm beads; I made one of each. Make only one 25mm bead. When you string the necklace, alternate the patterns the same way on each side.

Prepare the wooden beads by painting all of them gold. I do this by squirting some acrylic paint in a small, shallow cup of aluminum foil. I roll the beads in the paint with a toothpick until they are completely covered. Then I hang each bead on a toothpick inserted in the edge of a corrugated cardboard box to dry.

End and add thread by sewing 2-3 crossing diagonals to anchor the thread, as shown in "Peyote Window Bracelet" on pages 15 - 18. Do not tie knots because they could interfere with lacing the bead cover onto the wooden bead.

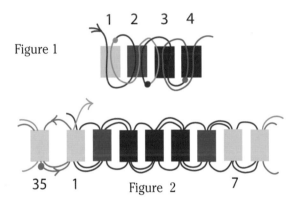

Figure 1

Figure 2

Figure 3

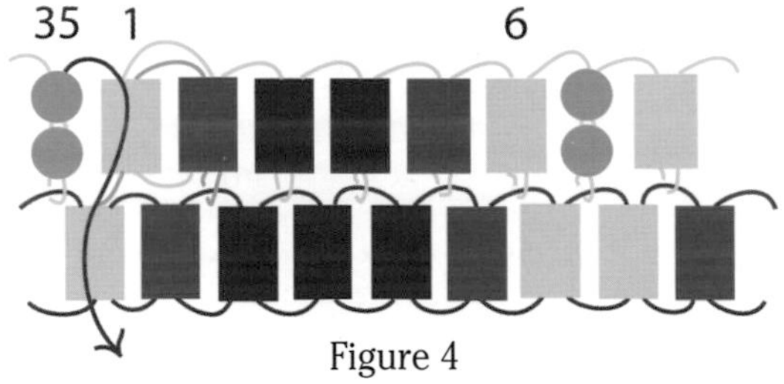

Figure 4

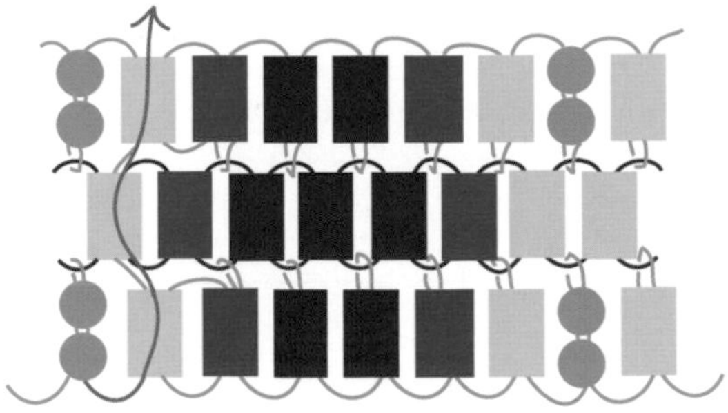

Figure 5

## Beads Used: Triangles • Rounds

### SUPPLIES

Wooden beads (one 25mm, four 20mm, six 16mm, six 14mm, four 10mm)
22 Stone rondelles, 8mm (I used aquamarine)
Large, bronze hook clasp (Ashes to Beauty Adornments)
2 Gold-filled crimp tube beads, 2 x 2mm
Flexible beading wire, 28-30" (71-76cm), 21- or 49-strand, size .014 to .019
Beading thread, One-G, dark brown and tan
Beading needles, sizes 10 and 12 or 13
Crimping or chain-nose pliers, Wire cutters
Gold acrylic paint, Toothpicks, Corrugated cardboard box
Red beads
    20-30g Triangles, size 11/0 (11T223, new bronze)
    20g Triangles, size 11/0 (11T222, bronze copper)
    20g Triangles, size 11/0 (11T951, bright coral/amber)
    20-30g Seed beads, size 11/0 (11R180,
        luster transparent green – looks like 270)
Green beads
    20g Triangles, size 11/0 (11T84F, matte metallic moss iris)
    20g Triangles, size 11/0 (11T24, silver-lined lime)
    20g Triangles, size 11/0 (11T270, forest green/amber)
    20-30g Seed beads, size 11/0 (11R222, bronze copper)

# Circular Brick Stitch

Start with a 20mm bead and make a ladder, repeating the 7-bead pattern five times (see pattern 1 for the 20mm beads, p. 33, top left). Note: the ladder is the middle, and longest, row on all the patterns.

1. To begin a ladder, thread a size 10 needle with 1½ to 2 yd. (1.4-1.8m) of tan thread for these red beads. Work with single thread. String 1 bronze and one coral triangle, leaving a 4" (10cm) thread tail to be woven in later (figure 1, dark brown line at left).

2. Sew through the 2 beads again in the same direction (starting at the tail) and tighten the thread. Position the beads so they are vertical and side by side.

3. Then pick up a bronze-copper bead (figure 1, tan dot to dark brown dot). Sew up bead #2 (coral) and tighten the thread to bring the side of bead #3 against the side of bead #2. Sew down bead #3 so your needle is exiting the last bead added (figure 1, dark brown dot to brown dot).

4. Pick up bead #4 (bronze-copper) and sew down bead #3. Tighten the thread and sew back up bead #4.

5. Add odd-numbered beads as in step 3 and even-numbered beads as in step 4.

6. The pattern repeat of 7 beads is bronze, coral, 3 bronze-copper, coral, and bronze as shown in figure 2 (the bronze beads on each end of the strip start pattern repeat #2 and end #5). Repeat the pattern 5 times. You will have 35 beads and your ladder will begin and end with a bronze bead.

7. To join the ladder into a ring, make sure it is not twisted as you bring bead #1 around next to bead #35.

8. With your needle coming out the bottom of the last bead (figure 2, brown dot at left), sew up bead #1 – toward the starting thread tail – then go back down bead #35. Sew back up bead #1, coming out the same end as the starting tail (figure 2, green line and arrow).

9. On the 20, 16, and 14mm beads, work a circular row on each side of the ladder before beginning the diamond points.

10. To begin any row of brick stitch so no thread shows on the edge, pick up the first 2 beads of the row, in this case a bronze and a coral bead. Sew under the thread loops between the second and third beads on the row below from back to front (photo 1 – note: photos 1-9 show construction of the 25mm bead). Then sew back up bead #2 toward bead #1 (figure 3, green line to light green dot).

Continue through bead #1 and pinch the beads as you tighten the thread (figure 3, light green line). Again go through bead #2, still pointing toward bead #1 (figure 3, dark green line to dot). Jiggle the thread as you pull it tight to turn both beads so their holes are vertical.

11. Add the rest of the beads on the row one at a time. Pick up the new bead (#3 is bronze-copper) and sew under the next set of thread loops on the row below from back to front. Sew through the new bead toward the previous bead (figure 3, light green lines on right) and tighten the thread.

12. After you've added the sixth bead (bronze) to the thread loop between the coral and bronze beads on the row below, pick up 2 green seed beads and treat them like a single bead as you attach them to the thread loop between 2 bronze beads (figure 4 shows the pattern of row 2.

13. At the end of row 2, the last bead you add will be the pair of green seeds. When you've sewn back up the pair of seed beads to complete the stitch, join the end of the row to the beginning by sewing down the first bead. Continue down the bronze ladder bead from which you started (figure 4, dark brown line and arrow).

14. Turn the ring over and repeat row 2 on the other side of the ladder, making sure that the beads are placed correctly so the pairs of green seeds go over the loops between 2 bronze beads on the ladder. When you join the last pair of seeds to the beginning of the row, continue through the original ladder bead and the bronze bead at the beginning of the first row 2 (figure 5, brown line and arrow).

## Diamond Points

When the ring for your 20mm bead is 3 rows wide and you're exiting an edge bronze bead, it's time to begin working decreasing rows of brick stitch to build up the first point (figure 6, brown dot at center right).

1. Start the 5-bead row by picking up 2 beads, as described in step 10 above.

2. Add the remaining 3 beads of the row one at a time, as described in step 11 above.

3. Exiting the last bead added, begin the 4-bead row with 2 beads (figure 6, right-hand top edge). Turn the beadwork so you can work in a comfortable direction.

4. The three bead row begins on the left side with 2 beads as usual.

5. Work the 2 bead row as in step 10 above, but when you sew back up the second bead, sew down the first bead again and continue down the bronze beads on the outside, right-hand edge of the triangle you've created. Continue through the bronze edge beads of the three ring rows (figure 6, brown line at right and photo 2).

6. Add the four decreasing rows on the other side of the ring to complete the first diamond (figure 6, right side bottom).

7. To get to the starting point for the next diamond, sew up the left-hand edge of the bottom point of the first diamond. Continue through the bronze edge bead on the ladder. Turn and sew down the next ladder bead and through the bronze beads in the ring on the right-hand edge of the next diamond (figure 6, light brown line to arrow). Make the bottom point first. Then follow the dark brown line up the left-hand side of the triangle and ring to make the top point.

8. If you were to sew down the bronze beads where you end up at the top of the second diamond, you'd be on the wrong edge to begin the third diamond, so turn and go down diagonally one bead in from the left-hand edge to the far edge of the ring. Then turn and go up the edge of the ring to work the top triangle of the third diamond first as shown (figure 6, green line to arrow).

9. You will have to make a similar turn to begin the fourth and fifth diamonds.

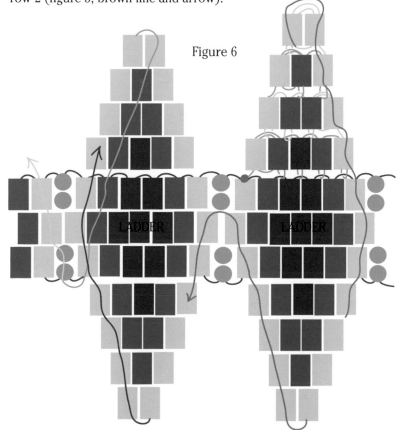

Figure 6

LADDER    LADDER

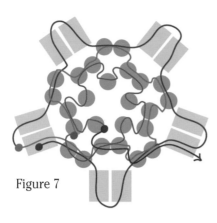

Figure 7

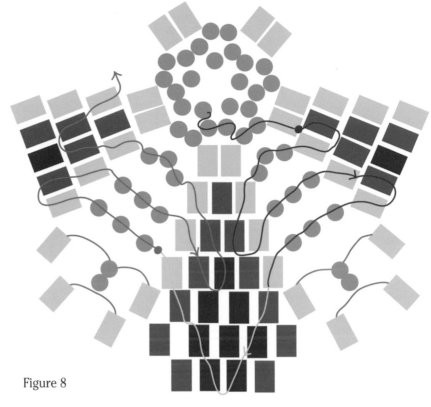

Figure 8

# Close the End

When you've completed the fifth diamond and your needle is exiting the second bronze bead, pointing away from the diamond, you're in position to close this end of the bead cover.

1. Pick up 2 green seeds and sew down the first bronze bead of the next top pair. Sew up the bronze triangle next to it and repeat around (photo 3) to make five arcs of 2 seeds each between the points (figure 7, dark brown dot to light brown dot).

2. Sew up the first bronze triangle and through the first pair of seeds again. Pick up 2 seeds and sew through the next pair of seeds on the previous round. Work a round of two-drop peyote stitch (photo 4 and figure 7, light brown dot to orange dot).

3. Connect the fifth pair of peyote seeds to the first arc and step up through the first pair of peyote seeds. Now peyote stitch 1 seed between each pair of seeds on the previous round (photo 5 and figure 7, orange dot to red dot).

4. Attach the fifth single bead to the first pair of peyote beads and step down through the second arc and the first triangle of the third point (figure 7, red dot to red arrow). (Note: do not sew through all the peyote beads of the last round to draw it tightly together as is normal.)

# Lace the Points Together

Don't insert the wooden bead yet. If some of the beads are hard to get through, use a size 12 or 13 beading needle.

1. Continue down the coral triangle in the middle of the 3-bead row (photo 6) then jog up through the bronze bead on the left-hand side of the third point (photo 7 and figure 8, upper right, red line to dark brown line).

2. Pick up 3 green seeds and sew down the bronze bead on the right-hand edge of the second point's 3-bead row. Continue diagonally down into the 4-bead row (photo 8) then up through the bronze bead on the edge of the row.

3. Pick up 3 seeds and sew down into the bronze bead on the edge of the third point's 4-bead row. Continue diagonally down into the 5-bead row. Then sew up the bronze bead on the edge of the row.

4. Pick up 3 seeds and sew down the bronze bead on the

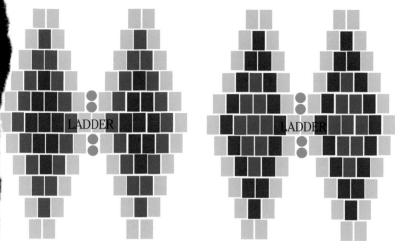

## 20mm Bead - Patterns for Color Variations

right-hand edge of the second point's 5-bead row (figure 8, dark brown line).

5. Continue diagonally down toward the middle of the second point through 3 more rows. Come up the adjacent bead on the other side of the center of the point and continue diagonally up through 3 more rows to exit the bronze bead on the left-hand edge of the second point's 5-bead row (figure 8, light green line to light brown dot).

6. Connect this edge of the second point to the right-hand edge of the first point with 3 sets of 3 seeds as shown (figure 7, light brown lines).

7. Then sew diagonally through the middle of the first point to begin connecting its left-hand edge to the right-hand edge of the fifth point as in steps 2-4.

8. Travel down then up through the fifth point as in step 5 and connect its other edge to the fourth point as in step 6.

9. Repeat step 7 to connect the fourth point to the open edge of the third point.

10. When you've joined the bottom row of 3 beads to the bronze bead on the right-hand edge of the third point, follow the bronze beads along the edge of the diamond to exit the 5-bead row on the other half of the diamond.

## Finishing the Beaded Bead

1. Insert the wooden bead in the half-joined bead cover with one hole centered in the completed peyote-stitch end.

2. Work the lacing in reverse starting at the 5-bead row (photo 9 – Note: on the 25mm bead shown, the bottom 2 lacing rows have 4 beads, instead of 3). Join the third diamond to the fourth, the fourth to the fifth, the fifth to the first, the first to the second, and the second to the third. Lacing is more difficult with the wooden bead inserted; you'll probably

be able to sew diagonally through only 1 bead at a time.

3. End by coming out one of the bronze beads on the tip of the third diamond. Then repeat the steps in "Close the End" to close the second end of the bead. Weave the thread through beads in the peyote end, tying 2-3 pairs of half hitches. Go through 2-3 beads before cutting off the excess thread.

4. To adjust the position of the wooden bead in the bead cover, insert the tip of your scissors into the hole and turn the wooden bead to center it.

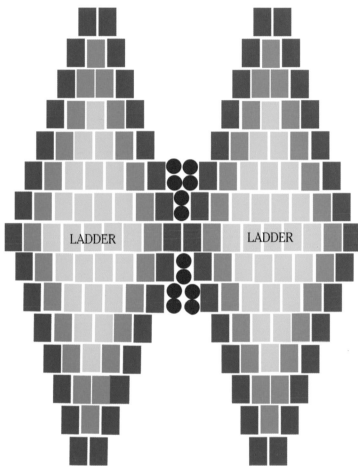

## 25mm Bead - Pattern for Colors

## Make the Other Bead Sizes

### 25mm Bead

1. Make one 25mm bead. There are 9 beads in each of the 5 repeats to complete the ladder.

2. Work two ring rows on each side of the ladder for a total of 5 ring rows.

3. Each point has 5 rows, beginning with a 6-bead row.

4. Close the ends as you did the 20mm beads, using bronze-copper seeds.

5. Lace the 3- and 4-bead rows of the points together with 3 bronze-copper seeds, but use 4 beads to lace the 5- and 6-bead rows together. You'll have to stitch diagonally down then up a row further than you did on the 20mm bead to get to the other side of a point.

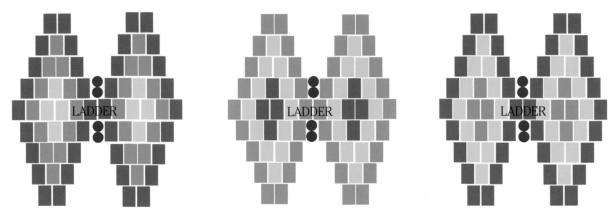

## 16mm Bead - Patterns for Color Variations

## 16mm Bead

1. Use the green palette for the 16mm beads and make 2 beads in each of the 3 patterns. The ladder has 30 beads, 6 for each of the 5 repeats.

2. There are 3 ring rows as on the 20mm bead, but there are only 3 point rows. The first has 4 beads.

3. When you close the end, begin by making 2-bead arcs between the points as on the 20mm bead, but work the 2 rows of peyote stitch with only 1 bead per stitch.

4. You have only 2 lacing rows between points. Add 2 seeds on the upper row and 3 on the lower row.

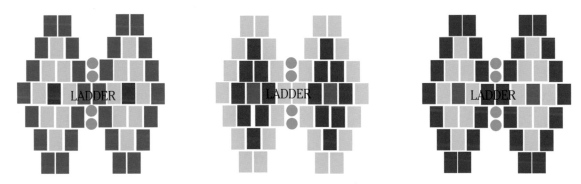

## 14mm Bead - Patterns for Color Variations

## 14mm Bead

1. Use the red palette for the 14mm beads, making 2 beads in each of the 3 patterns. The ladder has 25 beads, so there are 5 beads in each of the 5 repeats.

2. There are 3 ring rows, as on the 20- and 16mm beads. This means that there will be only 2 point rows on each side of the ring and that the first row will have just 3 beads (photo 10).

3. Close the ends as on the 16mm beads.

4. There is only one lacing row between points and it has 3 beads.

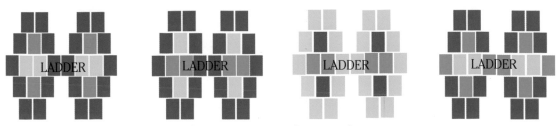

## 10mm Bead - Patterns for Color Variations